Internment

For Christian, be brave
and humble,
Love Mom.

Contents

Anosmia

Mi sentido falta
Un resultado de suelo contaminado o salado
Hojas comidas por mi madre
Los Gases inhalados por mi padre
Años de confinamiento
Quietud
Ruidos fuertes
Rocas en mi espalda
Pone en el ferrocarril pistas
La distancia del riel al suelo permite
El ajuste exacto de mi cuerpo
Tren pasa encima
No te mueras.

Anosmia

My missing sense
A result of contaminated or salted soil
Leaves eaten by my mother
Gases inhaled by my father
Years of confinement
Stillness
Loud Noises
Rocks on my back
I lay on the railroad tracks
The distance from rail to ground allows
The snug fit of my body
Train passes over
I do not die .

Ringleader

6 carats in a floral shape
Too pretty to wear daily
Cocktail style
Etched in Hebrew
Undefined Quality
Protected in an antique chest
Bartered for shelter
Under contract
Services declined

For I the LORD thy God will hold thy right hand, saying unto thee, Fear not; I will help thee. Isaiah 41:13

Immaculado

Intocable, yo escapo la muerte
como un borracho confuso
En el volante de un auto,
Y no le temo.

Consciente un cuerpo divino
Revolotea sobre mi piel rebelde,
Yo eludo la advertencia.

Yo espero concebir,
Buscando un pueblo
alimentado de pescado y pan.
Yo soy un milagro.

Immaculate

Untouchable, I escape death
like a confused drunk
at the wheel of the car.
I do not fear it.

Aware a Divine Body
Hovers over my rebellious skin,
I avoid warnings.

I await conception,
Looking for a town
fed by fish and bread.
I am a miracle.

Tunnel Wars

Smuggled with intricacy
Or crippled from machines
Concealed
Layered
Pinned
Blueprints in Golden Frames
Auctioned in the dark

Destabilize

One-legged is the cube l work in.
Weakened by routine
desensitized peers
unable to feel the pain of the petitioner
Tied down by regulations
some unread in years
summarizing
forgetting
ignoring exceptions to the exclusion
Inclusion time managed
by an aged digital watch
Reinvented to metal wreckages
instead of partitioned foam and cloth

Terror

Psychological warfare in the suburbs of Chicago
My boutique blouse ripped
Bruises underneath my cashmere sweater
Too many undiagnosed blows to the head.
Metal plates that dangle from the neck
and brace the knee
The imbalance slipped in between the cracks
Fighting for a country that has not been declared his
Digging in the mud of Texas
Plowing through the streets of Illinois
Lost proof of advanced mechanical degrees
Burned in my fireplace
Uncertainty
Evocations
Recorded messages
Investigated
Reunion to his home land
were athletic medals were won
And land was inherited
A new Trust
Outside of the Grid
I sewed together my ripped blouse and tucked it in a box.

For you, God, tested us; you refined us like silver
Psalm 66:10

Scribbled Canvas

crayola creation
with a color cream
sugar snow sprinkles
on my canvas square
like my desktop
hat, black hiding rabbit
jumping slashes on my
rainbow collage
of perfectly pigmented faces
eyes so circular
ball to be painted red
cheeks, pudgy
shade of beach brown
sand spread across the room
for improvement

Stubbed Toe

Today I stubbed my toe
On the office door of the 14th floor
My nail began to bleed
I quit my job from all the pain
Uninsured, I fled to Mexico
There I bought an anti-fungal
The label was unmarked
But it healed my toe
It may have been flammable,
who knows?

Ensayos de prisión

Estoy en línea para tragar un
suave-plata metal blanco.
Hemos aislados para medir
nuestro estado de ánimo.
Hoy en día sufría de frecuentes temblores
sobre todo mientras yo dormía.
Bebí jugo de arándano rojo muy concentrado.
Me salté el comer cualquier alimento sólido.
En huelga de la injusticia
Y el tono de voz,
Encendido porras
Empujado duramente en una esquina
En el manguito mis manos inocentes.

Prison Trials

l am standing in line to
swallow a soft- silver white metal.
We have been isolated to measure our mood.
Today l suffered from frequent tremors
mostly while l slept.
l drank highly concentrated cranberry juice.
l skipped eating any solid food.
On strike from injustice
And tone of voice
Lighted batons
Pushed harshly in a corner
To cuff my innocent hands

Missionary

Forged Geometry built these walls
By a man using bi-location in his portfolio
I only took the picture
The walls still crumbled
Because our books do not match
My simple phrases did not trick them
I bared too much skin
My head was not covered in the finest linen
My eyes were painted hazelnut
I knelt to the ground

May there be peace within your walls and security within your citadels. Psalm 122:7

Serenity

l wanted to understand her religion
but she had been quarantined for too long.
The science l learned as a child was expired.
There was no changing her mind.
She had already seen the underground channels
far before they became famous.
She just wanted to breathe
the oxygen from her greenhouse.
lt was never packaged or concealed.
Her formulas came in Psalms
l listened for the first time in years.
lt was quite, free from contamination.

Deformity

Passed down from my mother
The water did not come filtered back then
mold on un-amended shower walls
asthmatic coughs
more frequent than my classmates
triggered by climate change
pulsating sting on my left cheek
not diagnosed as a stroke
unresolved

Forgiving

More than others
I understood the trauma
My emotional attachment was a given
The value of it appreciated over time
Satisfied with formed concrete
and collectibles
I delayed my need to love
until all parties were cured
My tolerance remains pure

Badge # 857

Jumped over the chain-link fence
In line with standard protocol
two comrades on the run near by
armed with adrenaline
quick hands release the fired weapon
6 inches from the temple
Telepathic headaches of his wife and girls
Re-polished boots to cover the pursuit
Home in time for supper
3 blocks from the chain-link fence he jumped over

Reflections: